A GREAT BIG WORLD   IS THERE ANYBODY OUT THERE?

ISBN 978-1-4803-8457-6

HAL•LEONARD®
CORPORATION
7777 W. BLUEMOUND RD. P.O. BOX 13819 MILWAUKEE, WI-53213

Visit Hal Leonard Online at
www.halleonard.com

ROCKSTAR

Words and Music by IAN AXEL
and CHAD VACCARINO

wan - na know why. _____

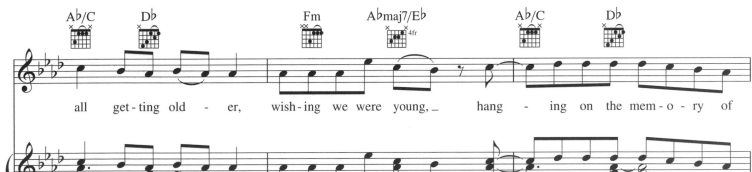

And we're

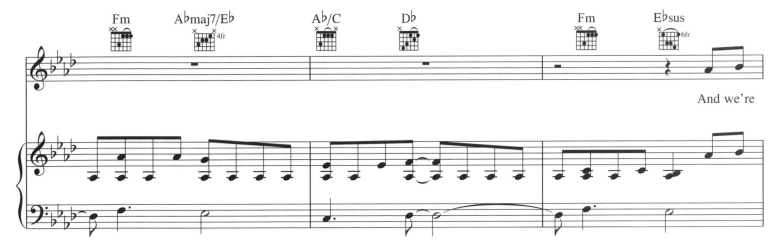

all get-ting old - er, wish-ing we were young, _ hang - ing on the mem-o-ry of

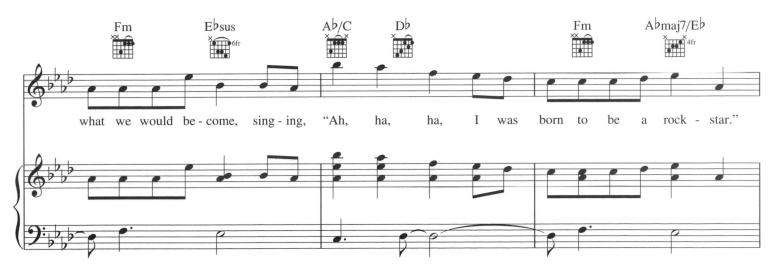

what we would be-come, sing-ing, "Ah, ha, ha, I was born to be a rock-star."

The more I look, it just gets hard-er to find. ____
I got a feel-ing that's what life's all a-bout. ____

The world is spin-ning, and I wan-na know why. ____
I'm learn-ing an-y-thing is pos-si-ble now. ____

Take a

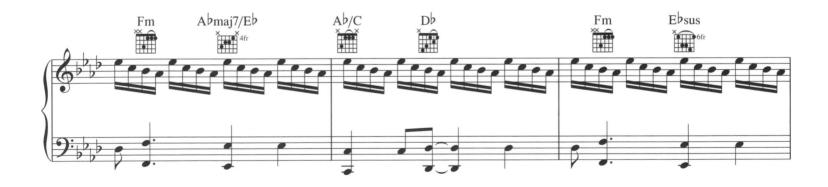

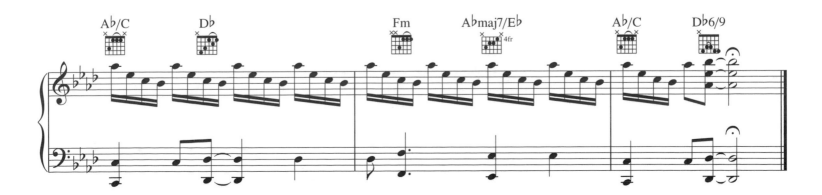

LAND OF OPPORTUNITY

Words and Music by IAN AXEL
and CHAD VACCARINO

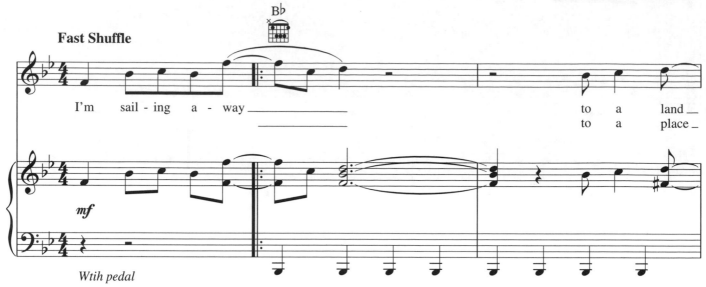

Fast Shuffle

I'm sail-ing a-way _____ to a land _
to a place _

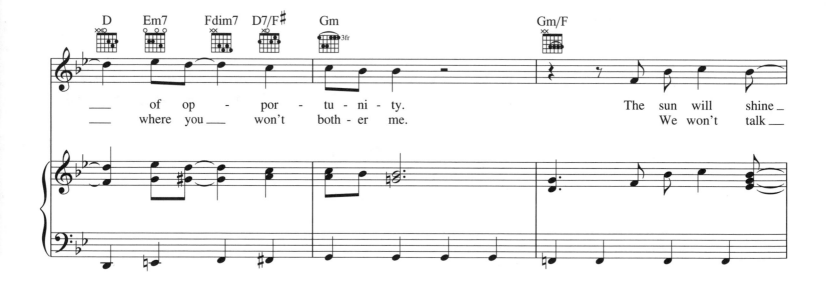

_ of op - por - tu - ni - ty. The sun will shine _
_ where you _ won't both-er me. We won't talk _

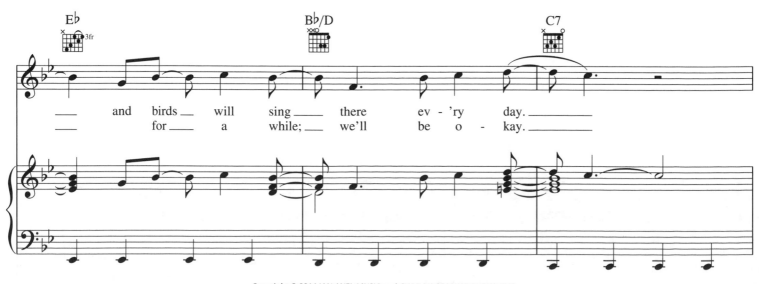

_ and birds _ will sing _ there ev-'ry day. _
_ for _ a while; we'll be o-kay. _

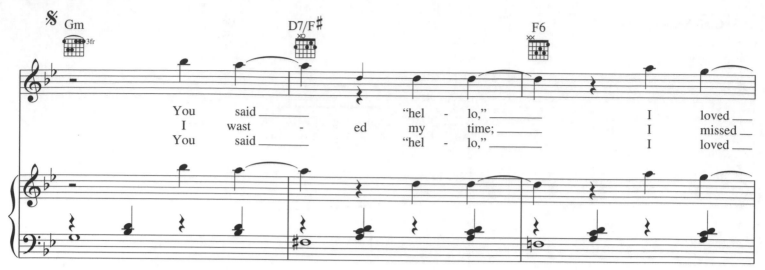

me.   Ah, _____   I just got - ta be - lieve, ___   I just got - ta be - lieve. _

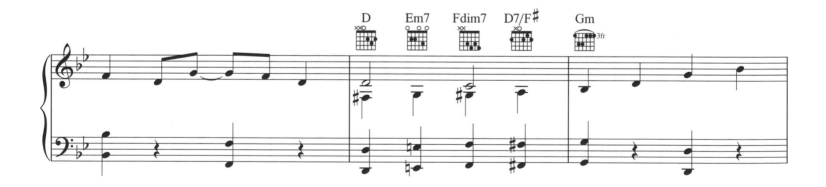

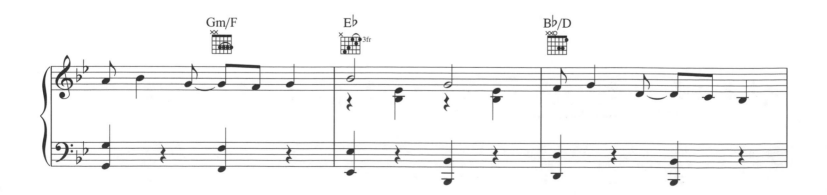

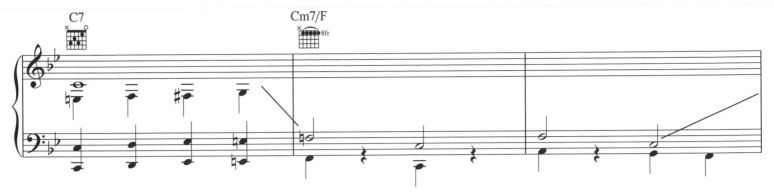

(Bup bah bup ba ba da ___ da ba ba ba,

bup bup bup bup ba da ba ___ da bup ba da

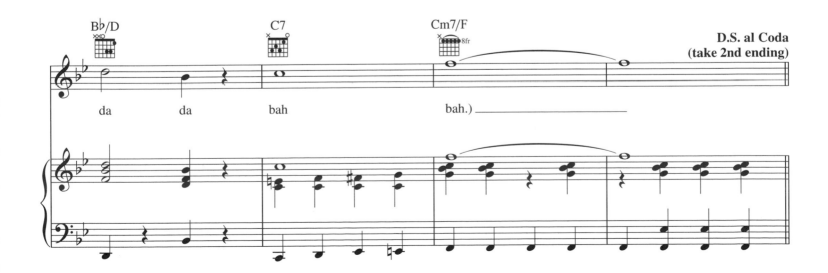

D.S. al Coda
(take 2nd ending)

da da bah bah.) ___

ALREADY HOME

Words and Music by IAN AXEL,
CHAD VACCARINO and HONEY LAROCHELLE

Moderately slow

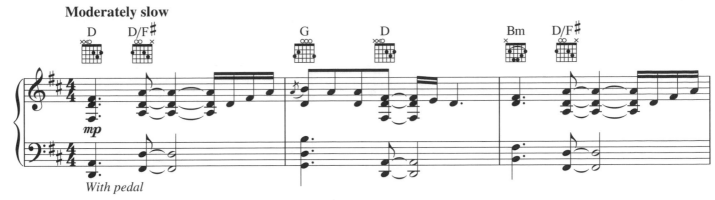

With pedal

You say ___ love is what you put in-to it.

You say ___ that I'm los-ing my will. ___ Don't you know ___ that you're all ___

___ that I think a-bout? You make up a half of the whole.

I'd prom - ise this cit - y won't get ___ in our ___ way. ___

___ When you're scared ___ and a - lone, ___ just know ___
And when you're scared scared ___ and a - lone, ___ just know ___

___ that I'm al - read - y ___ home. ___

When life ___ takes its own ___ course,

some - times _ we just _ don't get to choose. I'd rath - er be _

_ there next to you. Prom - ise you'll wait _ for me, wait _

_ for me, wait _ till I'm _ home. _

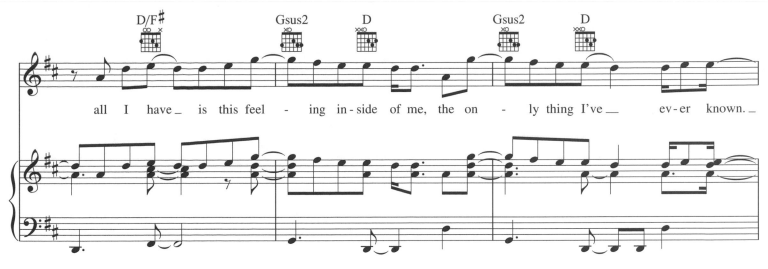

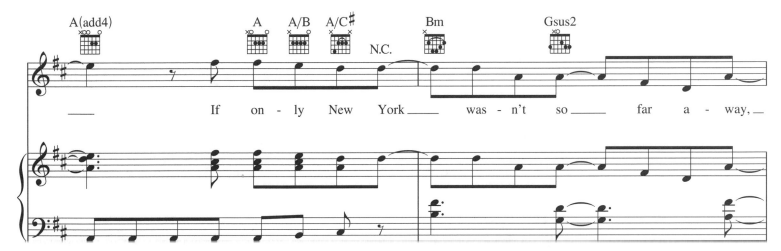

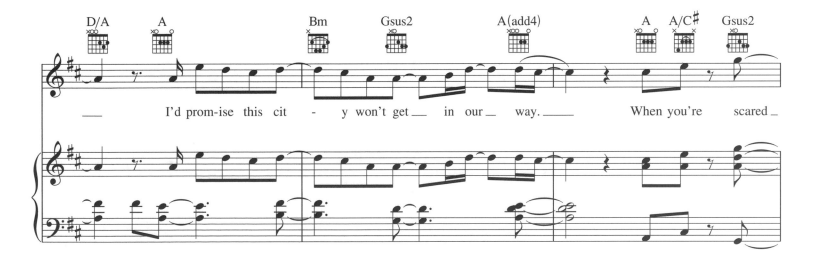

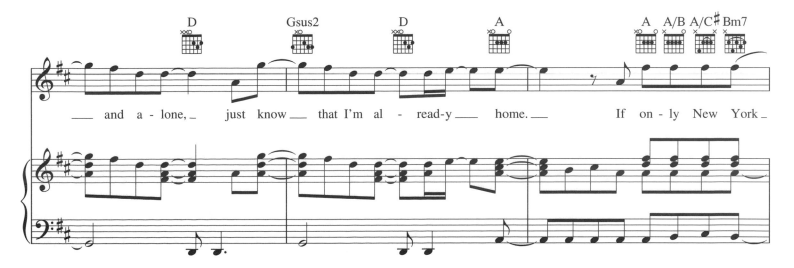

was-n't so far a - way. I will be there ev -'ry step of the way.

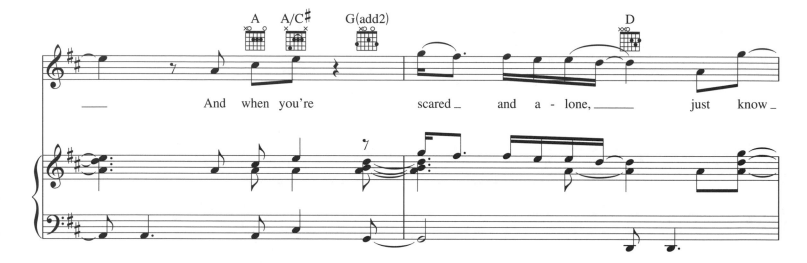

And when you're scared and a - lone, just know

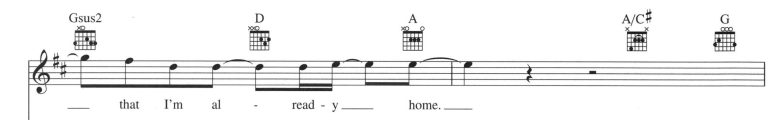

that I'm al - read - y home.

Just know that I'm al - read - y home.

I REALLY WANT IT

Words and Music by IAN AXEL
and CHAD VACCARINO

Moderately

So tell me, what are we liv-ing for?
If there's a mak-er up a-bove,

I say we chuck in-hi-bit-tions
Then why is no-bod-y lis-t'ning?

and sell our souls to rock and roll;
You show me hate, and I'll show you love;

*Recorded a half step higher.

I need to know what I'm miss - ing.
it's not a - bout your re - li - gion.

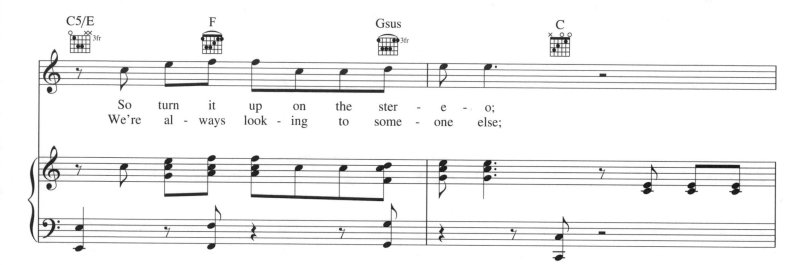

So turn it up on the ster - e - o;
We're al - ways look - ing to some - one else;

some - bod - y light the ig - ni - tion.
just take a look in the mir - ror,

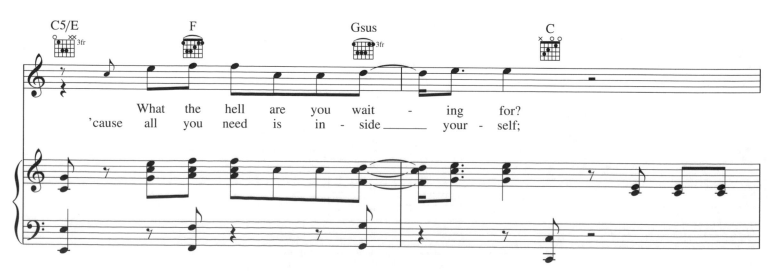

What the hell are you wait - ing for?
'cause all you need is in - side your - self;

It's time to make a de-ci - sion.
it could -n't be an - y clear - er.
Na

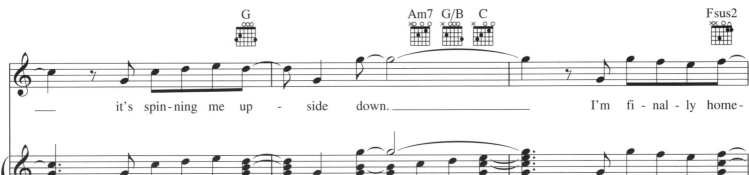

ooh, _____ I'm feel -ing the world __ go _____ 'round; _

__ it's spin-ning me up - side down. _____ I'm fi - nal - ly home-

- ward _____ bound. __ I'm not giv -ing up. It's crawl-ing un -der my skin, _

and I don't care if I sin, _____ I real-ly want it,

I real-ly want it, I real-ly want it right now.

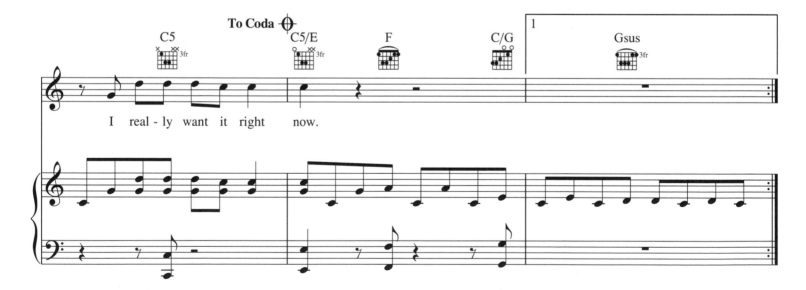

I real-ly want it right now.

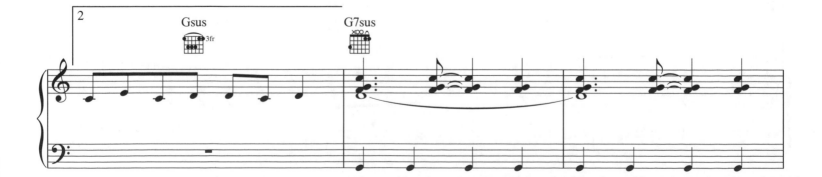

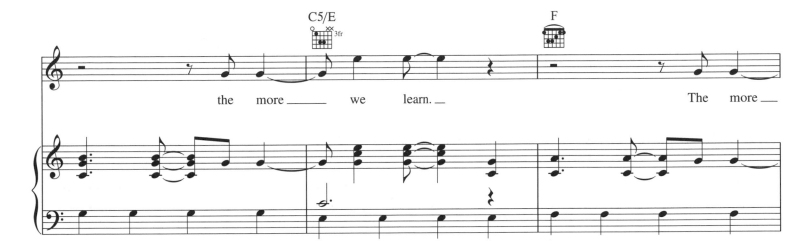

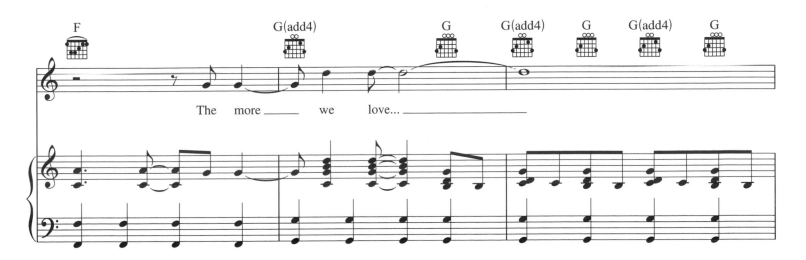

N.C.

Tell me, what are we liv - ing for? I say we chuck in - hi - bi -

- tions and sell our souls to rock and roll;

D.S. al Coda

I need to know what I'm miss - ing. Na

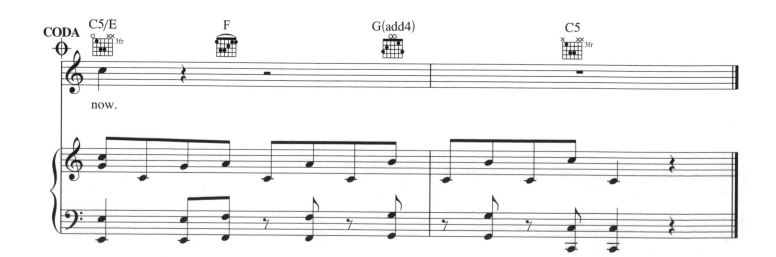

CODA

C5/E   F   G(add4)   C5

now.

SAY SOMETHING

Words and Music by IAN AXEL,
CHAD VACCARINO and MIKE CAMPBELL

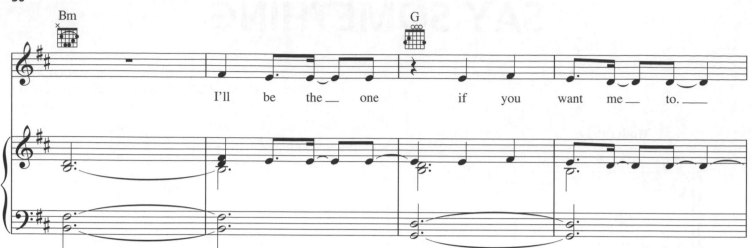

I'll be the __ one if you want me __ to. __

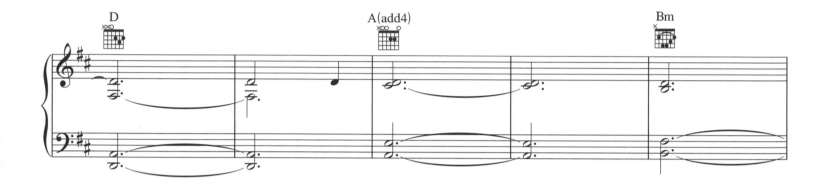

An - y - where __ I would have fol - lowed __ you. __

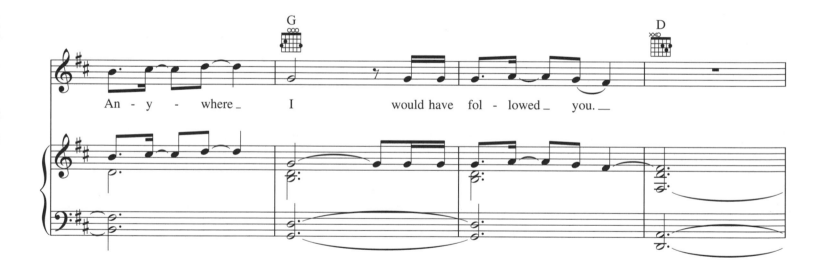

Say some - thing,

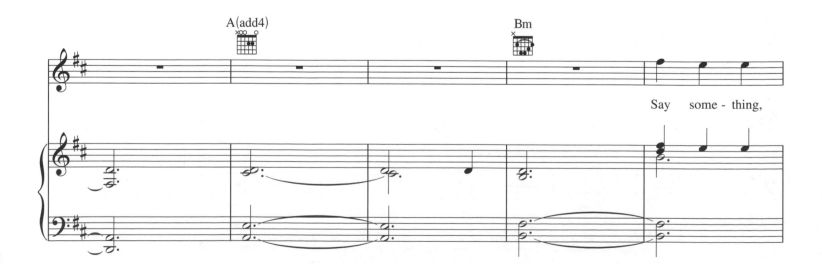

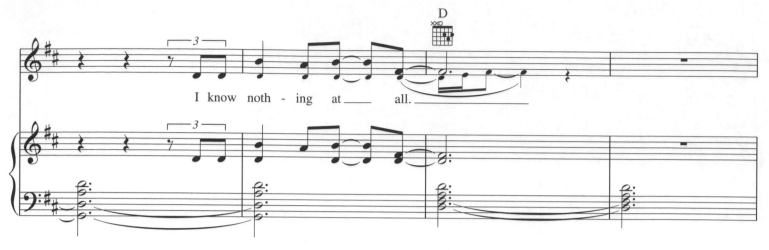

I know noth - ing at ____ all. ____

And I

will stum - ble and ___ fall.
will swal - low my ___ pride.

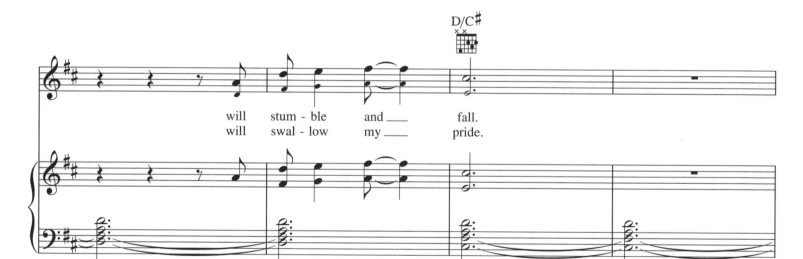

I'm still ___ learn - ing to love,
You're the ___ one ____ that I love,

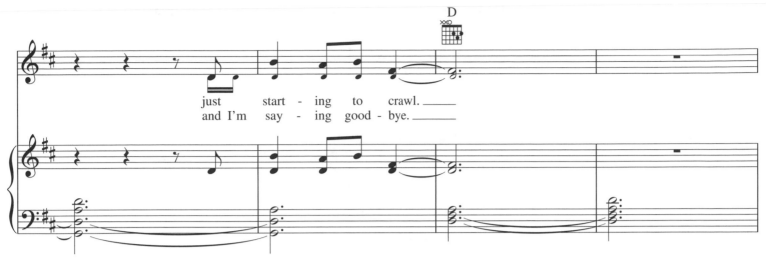

just start - ing to crawl. _____
and I'm say - ing good - bye. _____

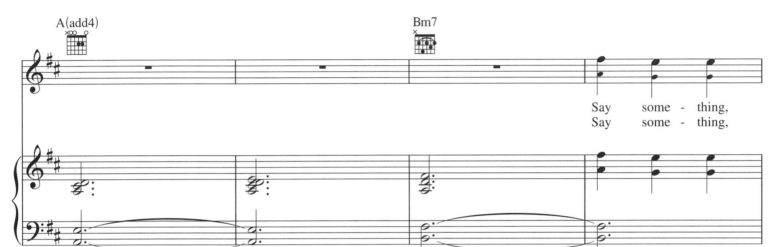

Say some - thing,
Say some - thing,

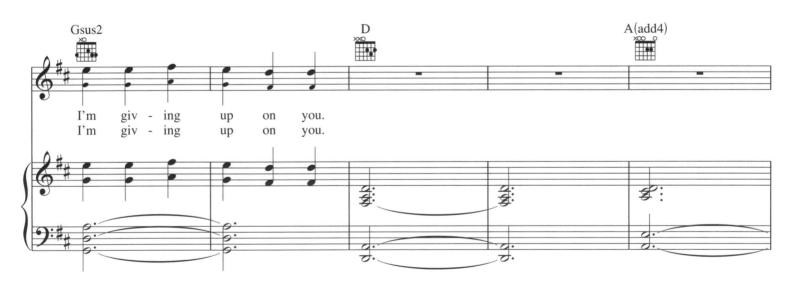

I'm giv - ing up on you.
I'm giv - ing up on you.

I'm sor - ry that I _____ could - n't _____ get _____
And I'm sor - ry that I _____ could - n't _____ get _____

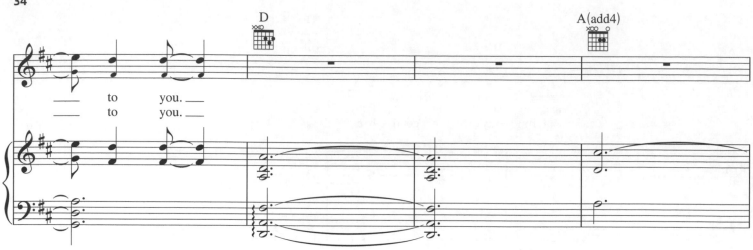

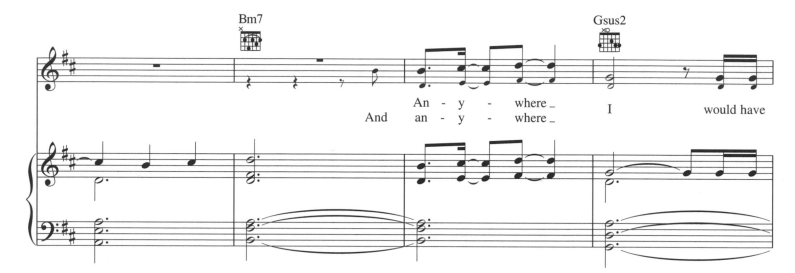

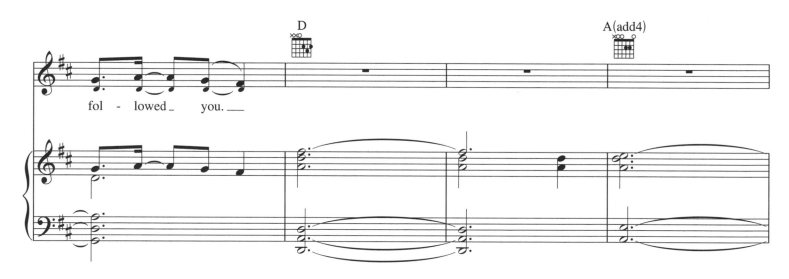

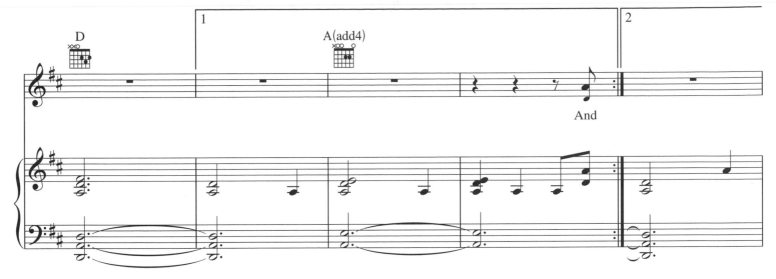

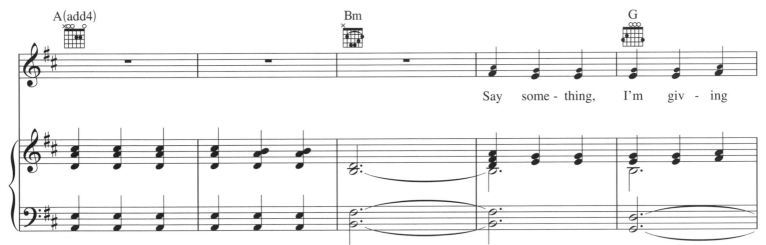

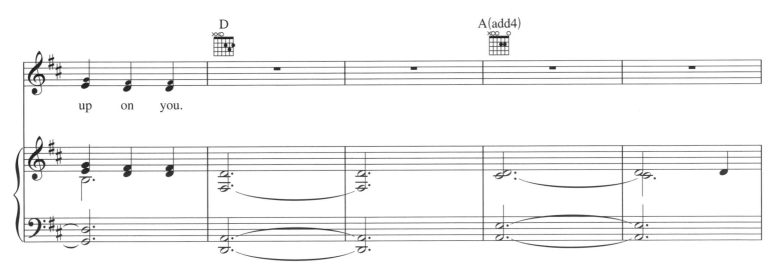

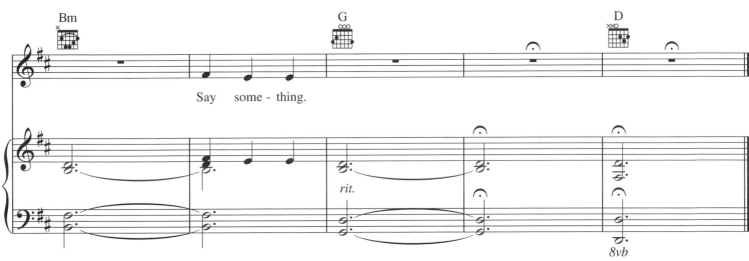

YOU'LL BE OKAY

Words and Music by IAN AXEL
and CHAD VACCARINO

Moderately slow Gospel feel

You'll be o - kay.
You'll be o - kay. _
You'll be o - kay. _

The sun will rise _____
Just look in - side; _____

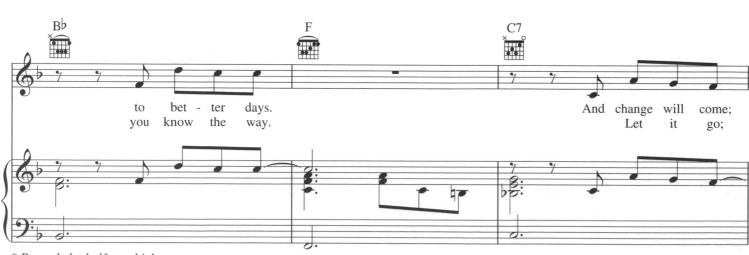

to bet - ter days.
you know the way.

And change will come;
Let it go;

* Recorded a half step higher.

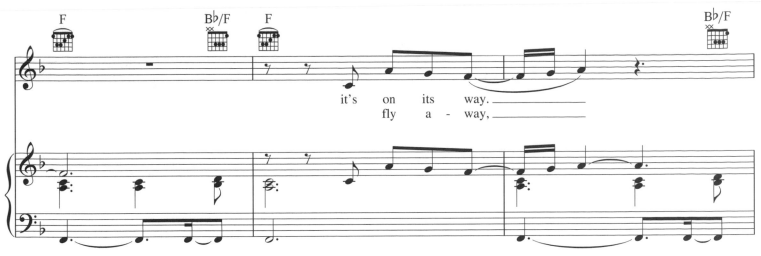

it's on its way. _____
fly a - way, _____

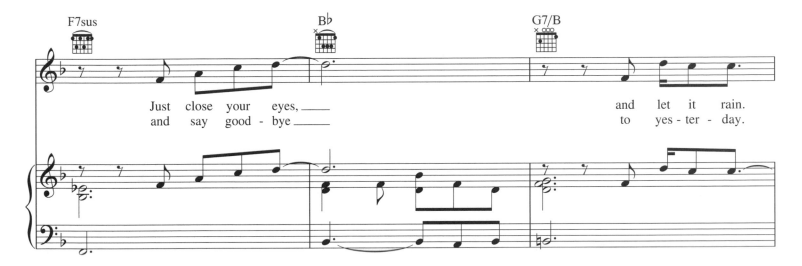

Just close your eyes, _____ and let it rain.
and say good - bye _____ to yes - ter - day.

'Cause you're nev - er a - lone,

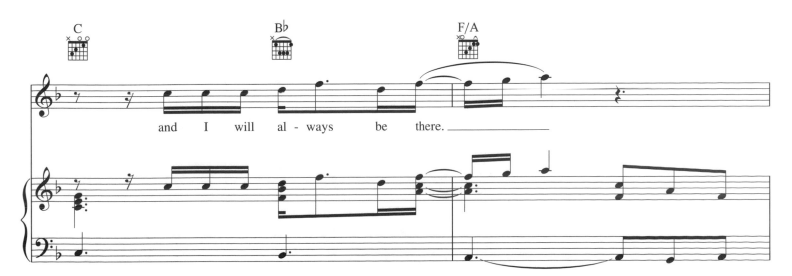

and I will al - ways be there. _____

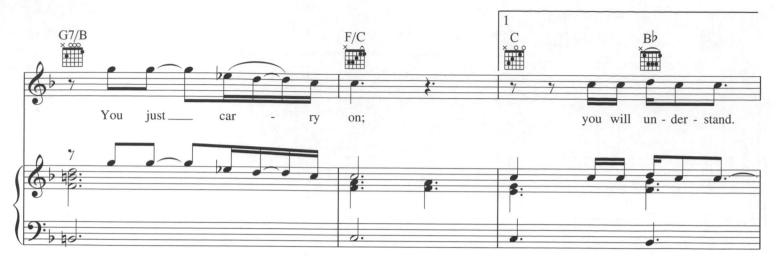

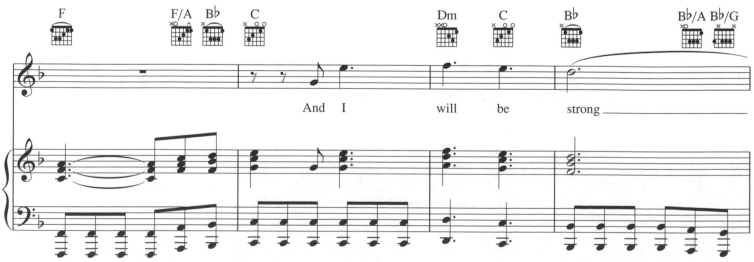

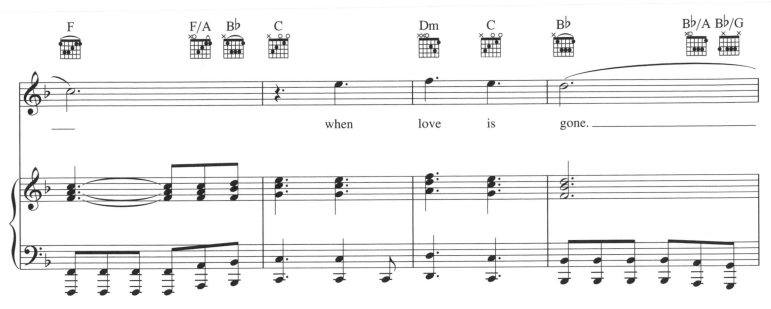

when love is gone. _____

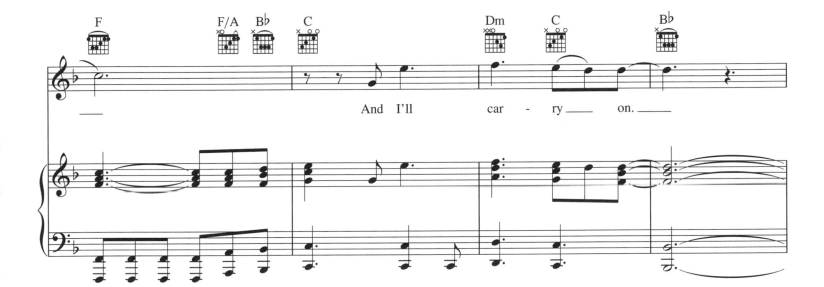

And I'll car - ry ___ on. ___

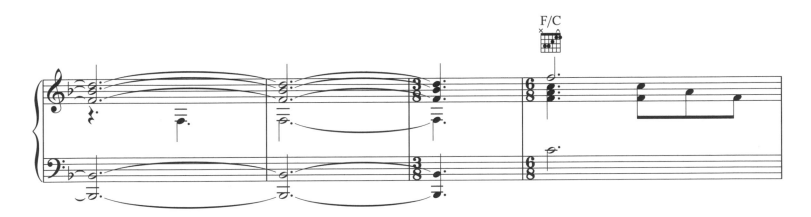

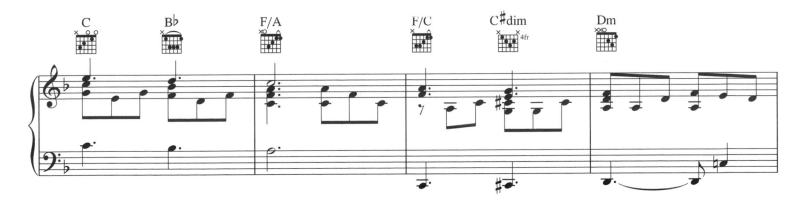

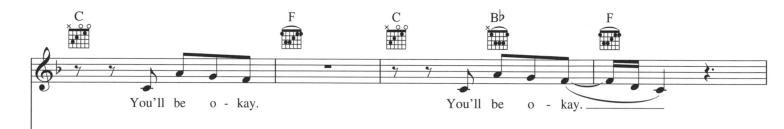

EVERYONE IS GAY

Words and Music by IAN AXEL
and CHAD VACCARINO

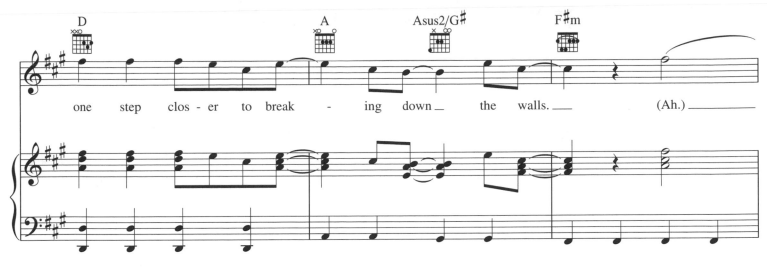

one step clos - er to break - ing down the walls. (Ah.)

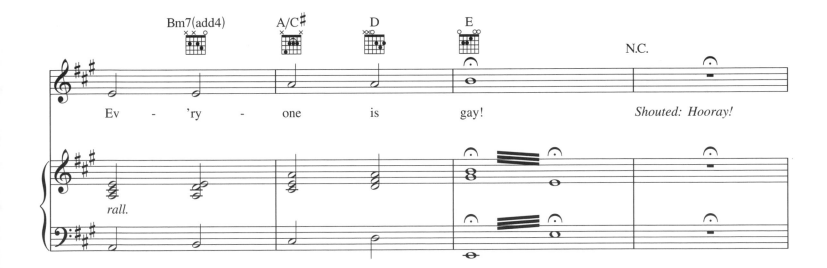

Ev - 'ry - one is gay! Shouted: Hooray!

rall.

a tempo rall.

THERE IS AN ANSWER

Words and Music by IAN AXEL
and CHAD VACCARINO

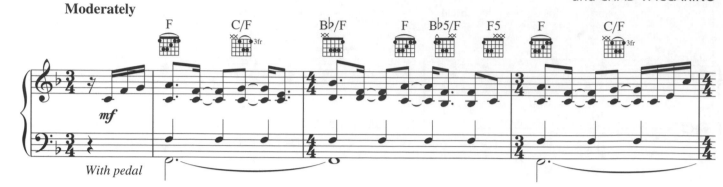

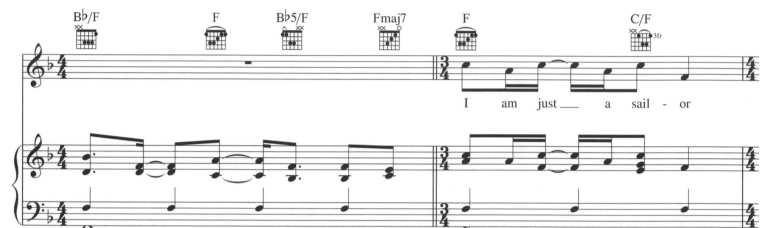

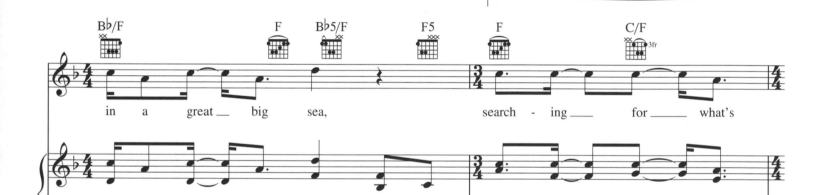

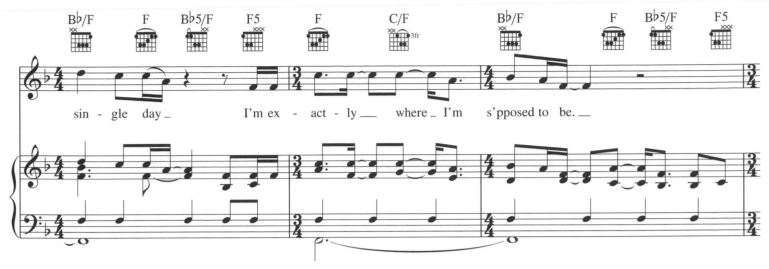

sin - gle day _ I'm ex - act - ly _ where _ I'm s'pposed to be. _

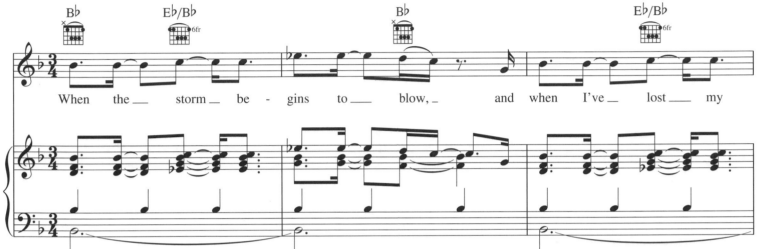

When the _ storm _ be - gins to _ blow, _ and when I've _ lost _ my

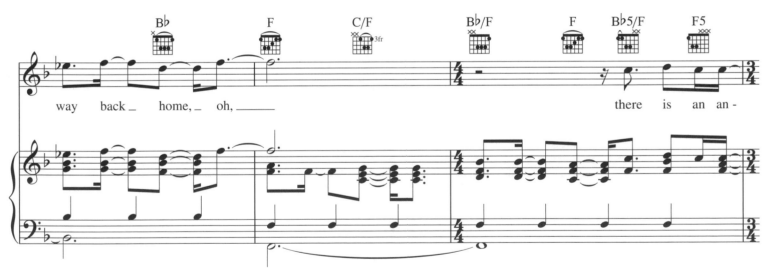

way back _ home, _ oh, _____ there is an an -

- swer. _ Oh, _____

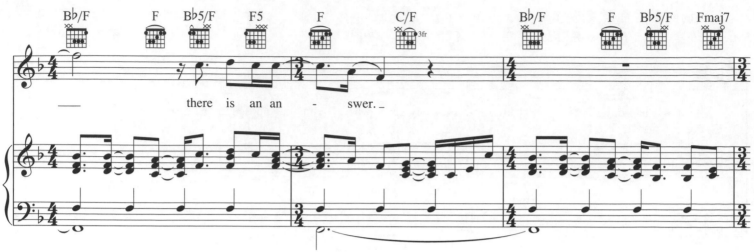

there is an an - swer.

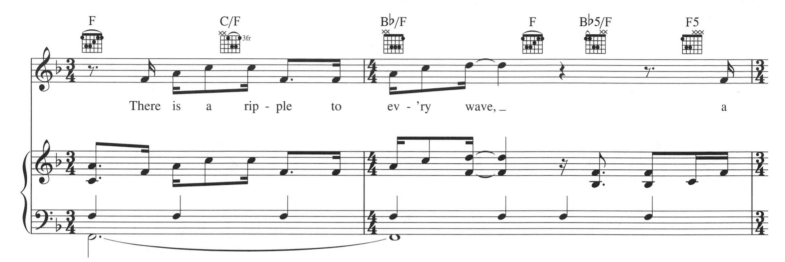

There is a rip - ple to ev - 'ry wave, ___ a

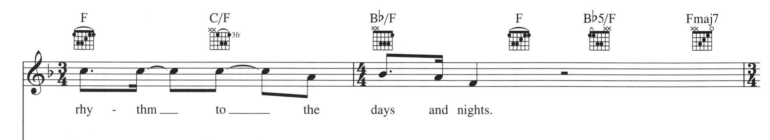

rhy - thm ___ to ___ the days and nights.

And all the thoughts ___ that make the world ___ go 'round, ___

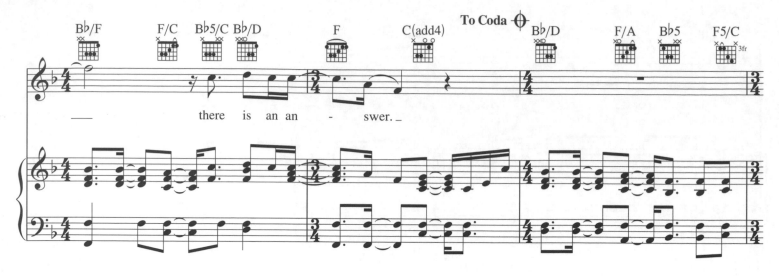

there is an an - swer.

There is no dif - f'rence be - tween you and me; ___ it

lies be - yond ___ our his - to - ry. ___

And if ___ we on - ly take the time to see, ___ we're all ___ we

D.S. al Coda

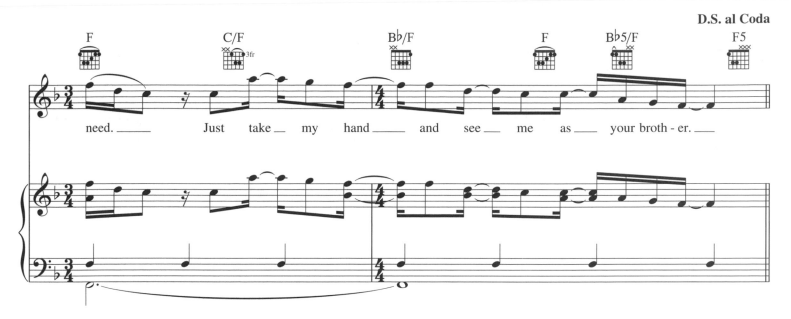

need. _____ Just take _____ my hand _____ and see _____ me as _____ your broth - er. _____

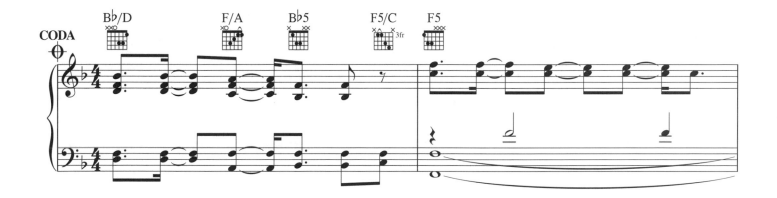

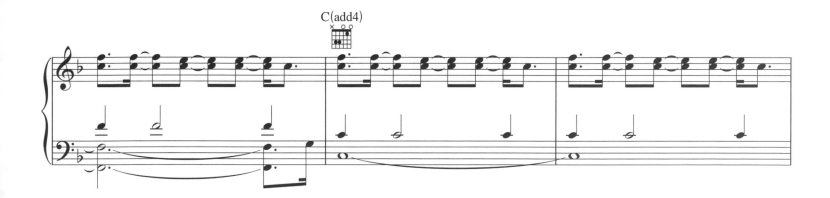

Near   or far, __

C(add4)   Dm7

_____   oh, I _____ be - lieve __ that love __

B♭sus2   F5

___ will find us there. ___   And through __

F   C7sus

___   the dark, _____

Oh I ___ be - lieve ___ that love ___ will find us there.

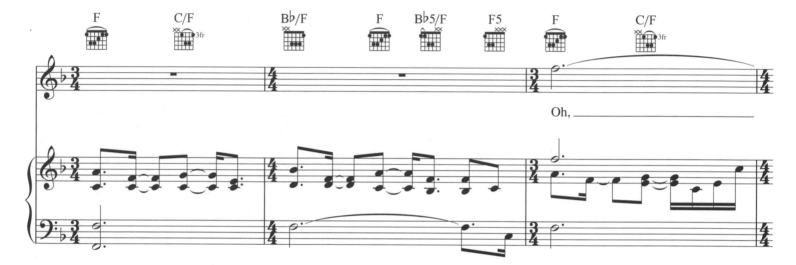

Oh, _____

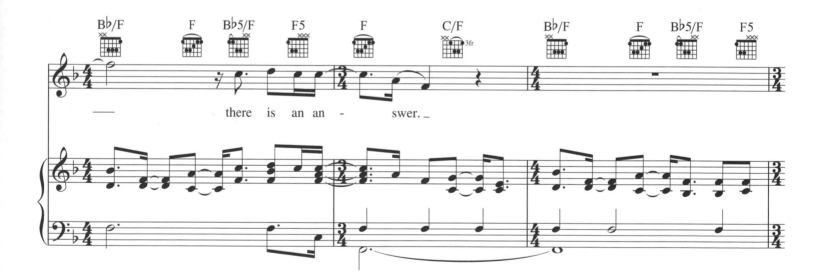

there is an an - swer. _

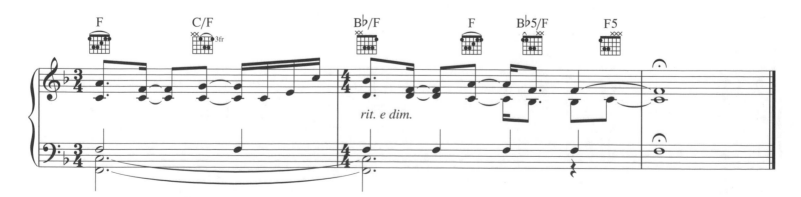

rit. e dim.

I DON'T WANNA LOVE SOMEBODY ELSE

Words and Music by IAN AXEL,
CHAD VACCARINO and ALLIE MOSS

The stars ___ had a - ligned; ___

I thought that I found ___ you. And

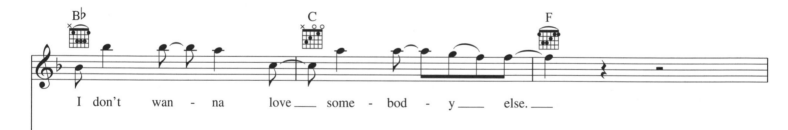

I don't wan - na love ___ some - bod - y ___ else. ___

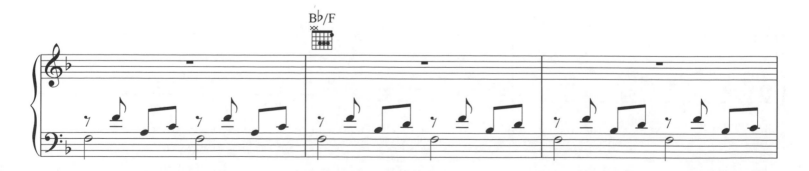

Oh, we left it all un-spok - en.

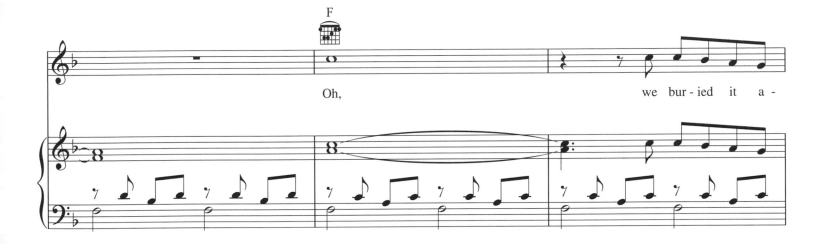

Oh, we bur -ied it a -

live, and now ___ it's scream - ing in ___ my head. ___

Oh,

I should-n't go on hop - ing, —

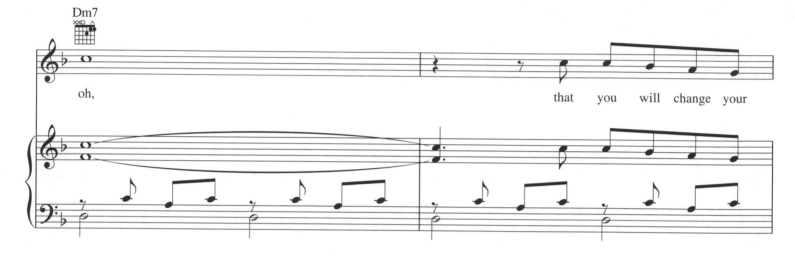

oh, that you will change your

mind, and one — day we — could start — a - gain. —

Well, I _____ don't care _____ if lone - li - ness kills _

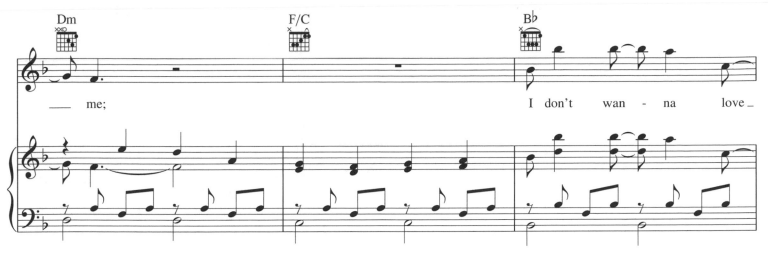

me;   I don't wan - na love _

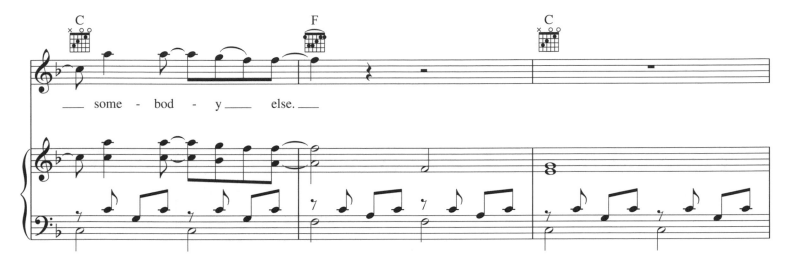

_ some - bod - y _ else. _

Ooh. _____

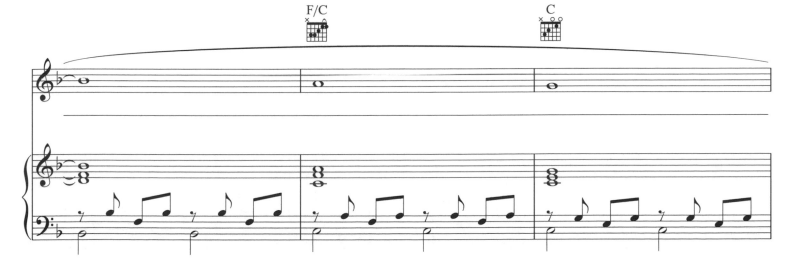

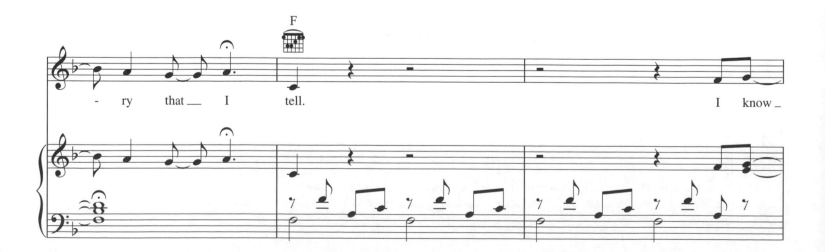

that it's time ___ to tell you it's o - ver,

but I don't wan - na love ___ some - bod - y ___ else. ___

No ___ ooh. _____

THIS IS THE NEW YEAR

Words and Music by IAN AXEL
and CHAD VACCARINO

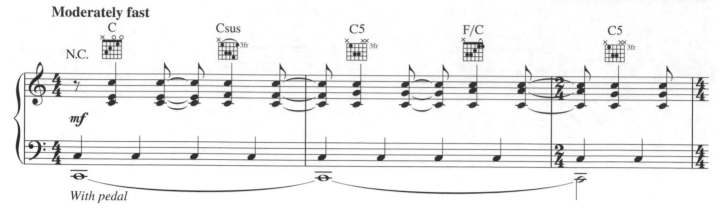

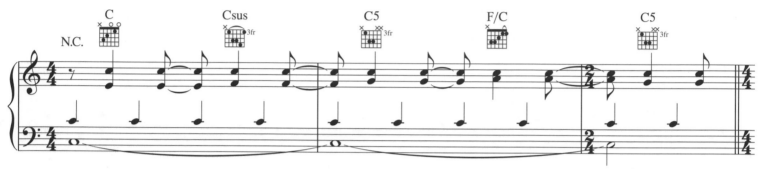

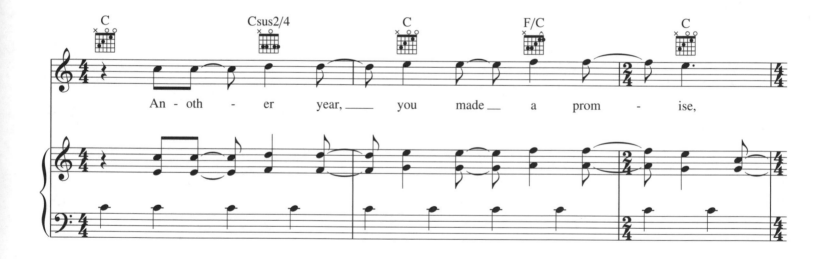

An-oth-er year,_____ you made_____ a prom-ise,

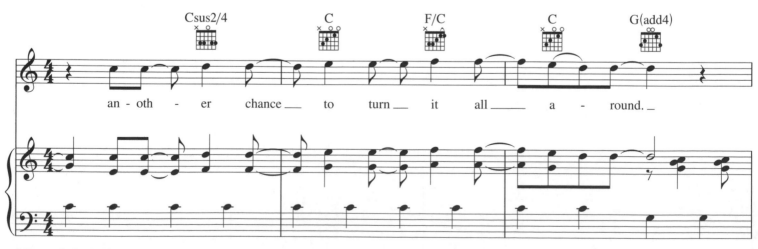

an-oth-er chance_____ to turn_____ it all_____ a - round._

* Recorded a half step lower.

And do___ not save___ this for___ to - mor - row;

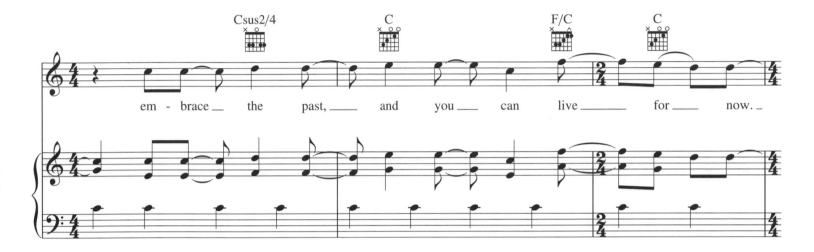

em - brace __ the past, ___ and you __ can live _____ for __ now. _

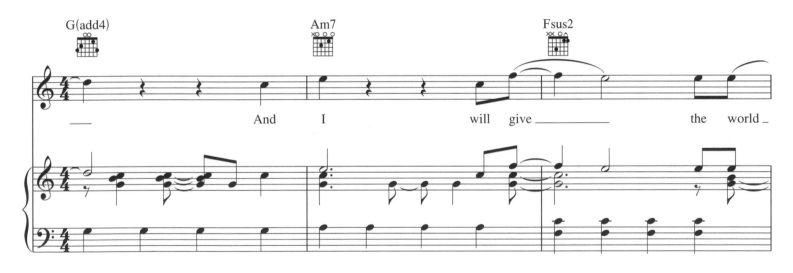

___ And I will give _____ the world _

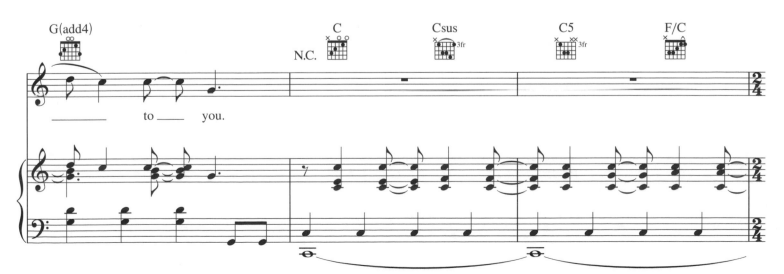

_____ to ___ you.

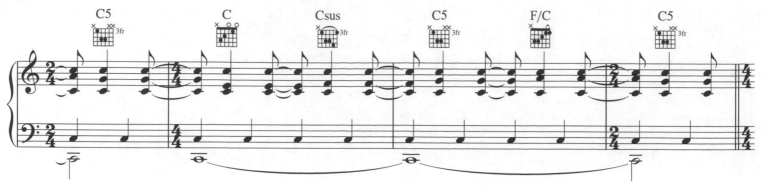

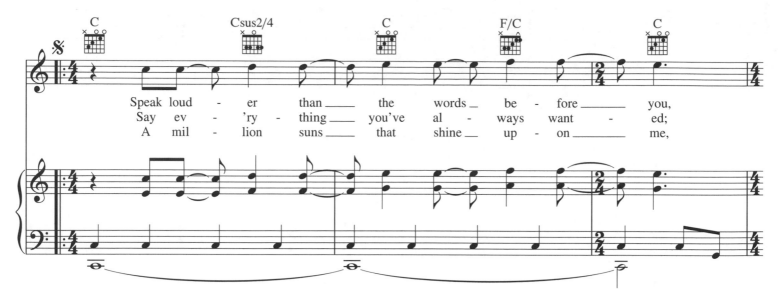

Speak loud - er than ___ the words ___ be - fore ___ you,
Say ev - 'ry - thing ___ you've al - ways want - ed;
A mil - lion suns ___ that shine ___ up - on ___ me,

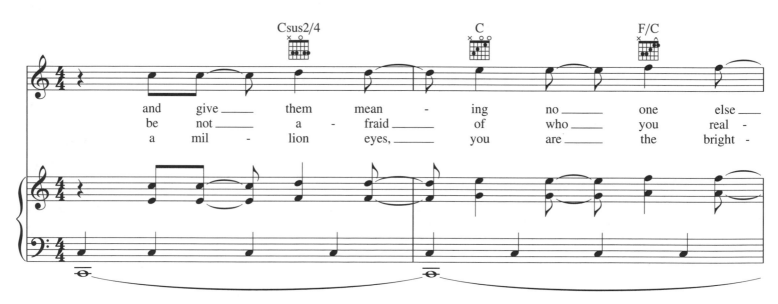

and give ___ them mean - ing no ___ one else ___
be not ___ a - fraid ___ of who ___ you real -
a mil - lion eyes, ___ you are ___ the bright -

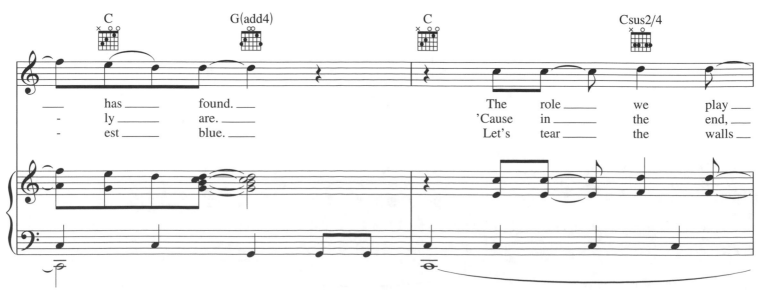

___ has ___ found. ___ The role ___ we play ___
- ly ___ are. ___ 'Cause in ___ the end, ___
- est ___ blue. ___ Let's tear ___ the walls ___

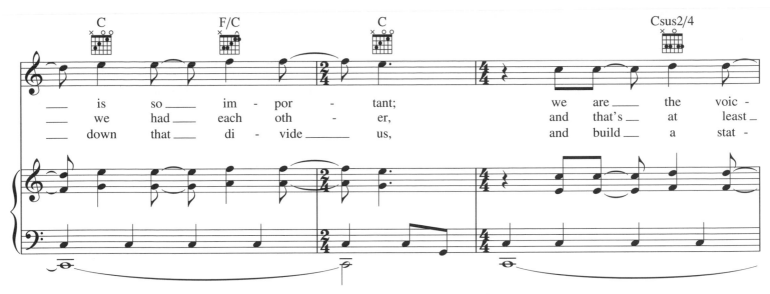

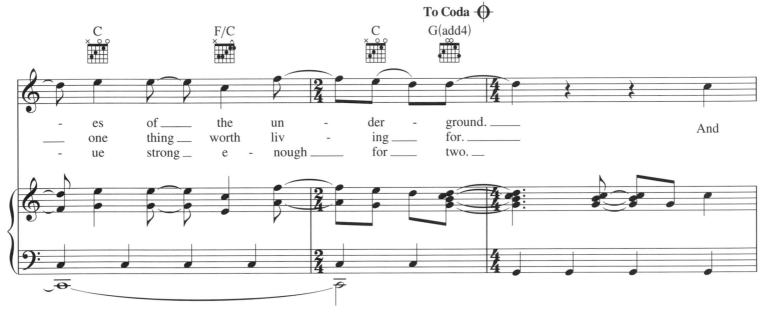

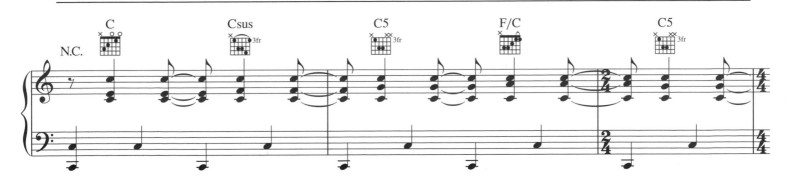

the world ___ to you. ___

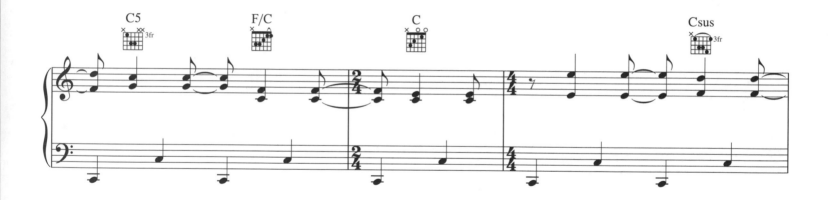

D.S. al Coda

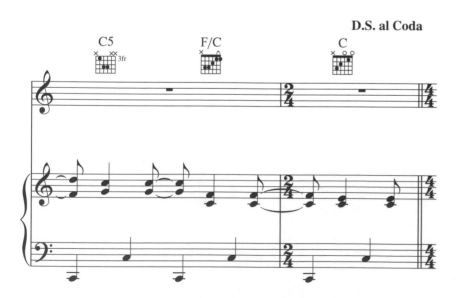

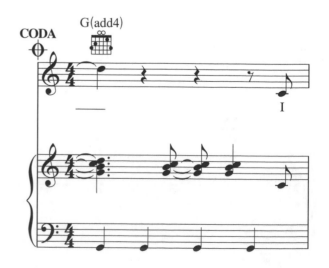

pass it back ___ to you. ___

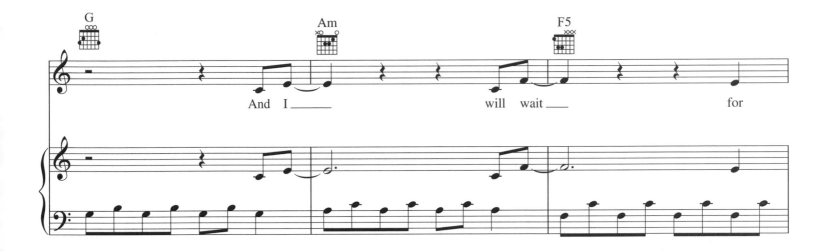

And I ___ will wait ___ for

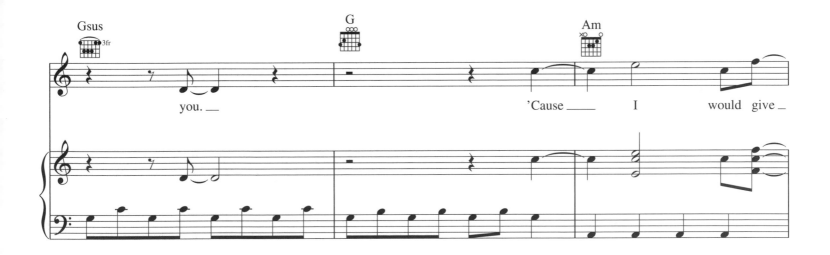

you. ___ 'Cause ___ I would give ___

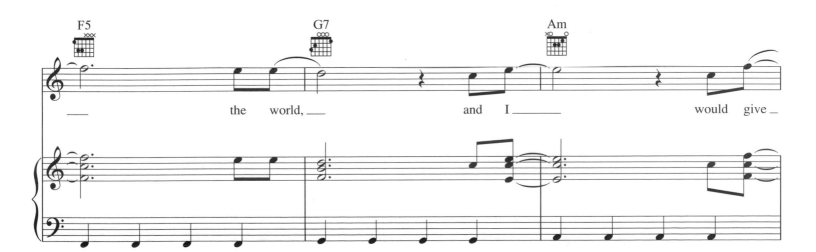

___ the world, ___ and I ___ would give ___

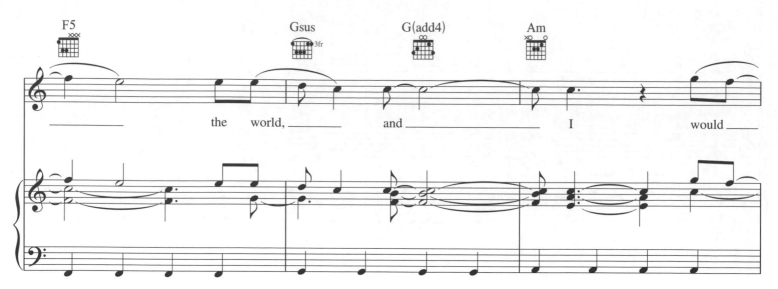

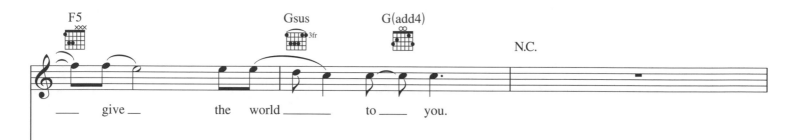

the world, _____ and _____ I would _____

give ___ the world _____ to ___ you.

This is ____ the new ____ year,
We are ____ the voic - es.

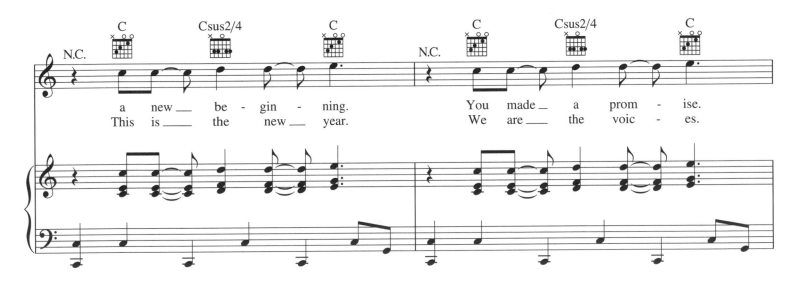

a new ____ be - gin - ning.
This is ____ the new ____ year.

You made ____ a prom - ise.
We are ____ the voic - es.

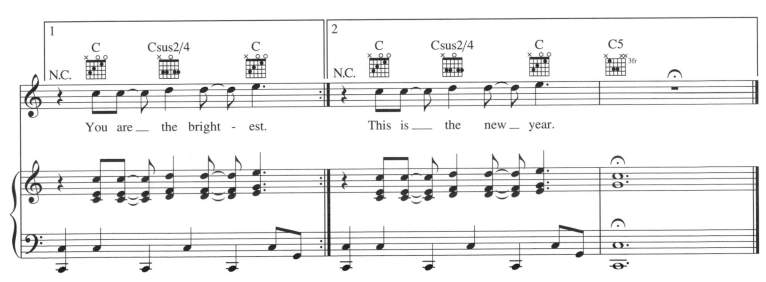

1
You are ____ the bright - est.

2
This is ____ the new ____ year.

SHORTY DON'T WAIT

Words and Music by IAN AXEL
and CHAD VACCARINO

Half-time Shuffle feel

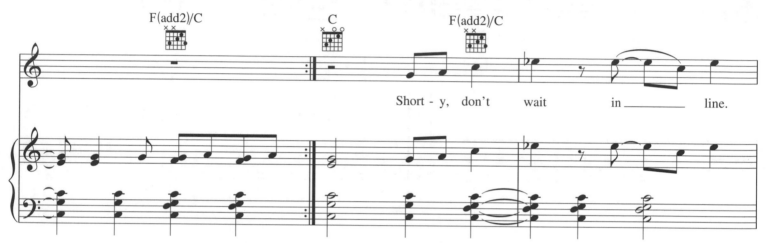

Short - y, don't wait in _____ line.

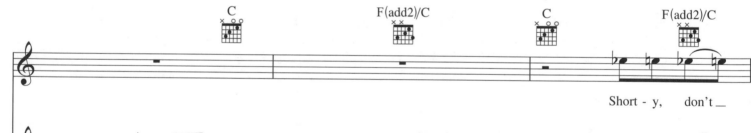

Short - y, don't _

wait till the sun _ don't shine. _

I'll be there _____ to give _____ you mine. _____
well, they ain't worth _____ your pre - cious time. _____
so you can rest _____ your head _____ on mine. _____

C   F/C   C   F/C   C   N.C.

And when you lose _
And when there's no _
And when you feel _

F(add2)

_____ that hap - py feel - ing,
_____ one you ___ can turn _____ to,
_____ like start - ing o - ver,

Am7   G5

Well, I will lift _____ your spir - its high. ___
I'll be right _____ there by _____ your side. ___
Well, don't think twice; _____ it's _____ al - right. ___

Yeah, it's __ al - right. __

(1.) So Short - y, don't
(2.) Short - y, don't
(3., 4.) Short - y, don't

wait in __ line.

Short - y, don't __ wait till the sun __ don't shine. __

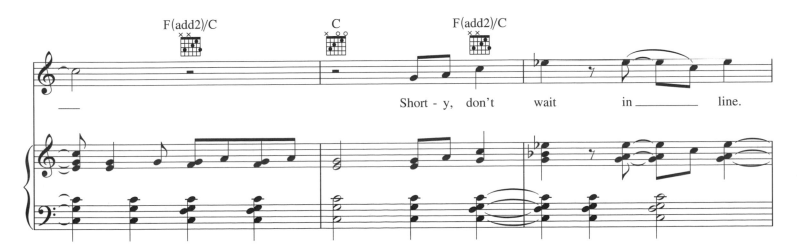

Short - y, don't wait in __ line.

CHEER UP!

Words and Music by IAN AXEL
and CHAD VACCARINO

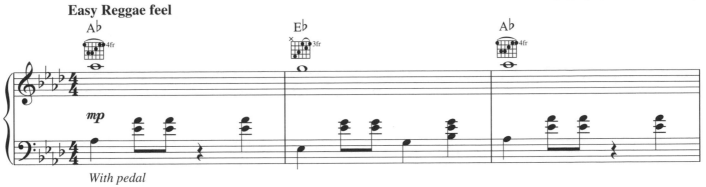

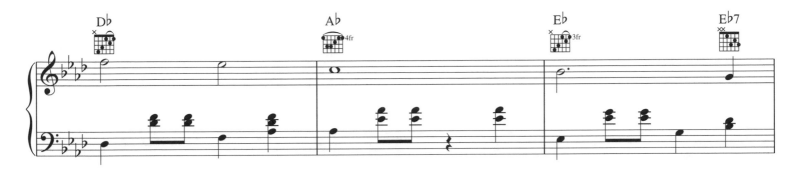

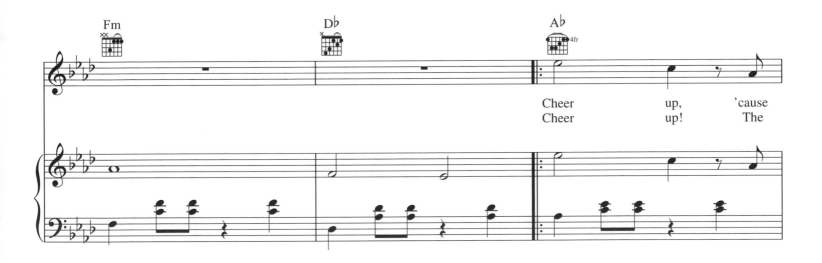

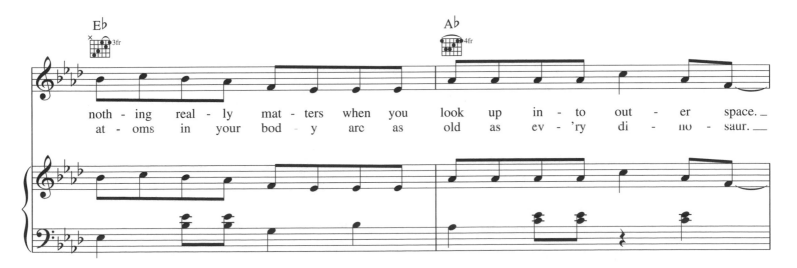

It's a great big world, and there's no need to
You're a spe - cial part of one big grand de -

cry. _____ Cheer up! We're
sign. _____ Cheer up! We're

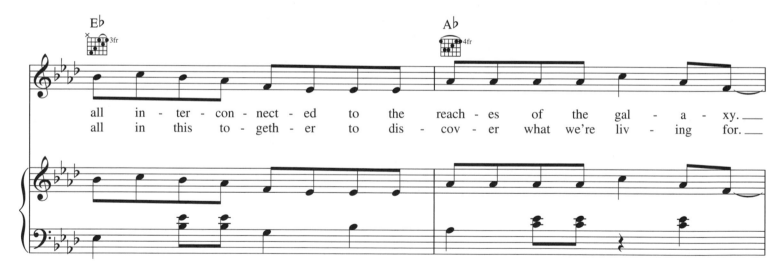

all in - ter - con - nect - ed to the reach - es of the gal - a - xy. ___
all in this to - geth - er to dis - cov - er what we're liv - ing for. ___

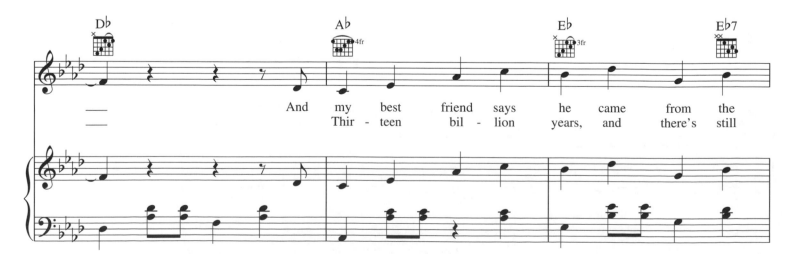

_____ And my best friend says he came from the
_____ Thir - teen bil - lion years, and there's still

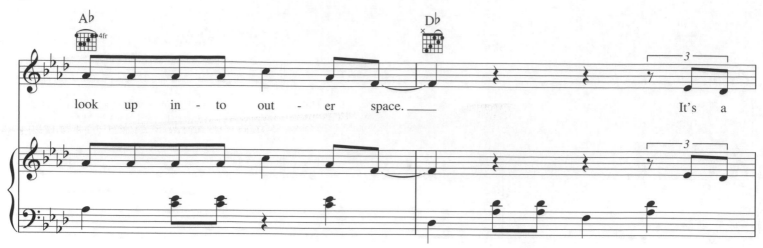

look up in - to out - er space._____ It's a

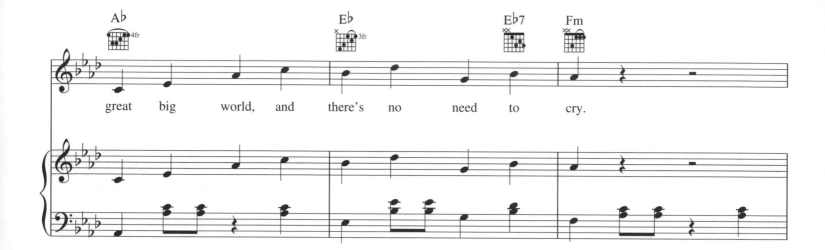

great big world, and there's no need to cry.

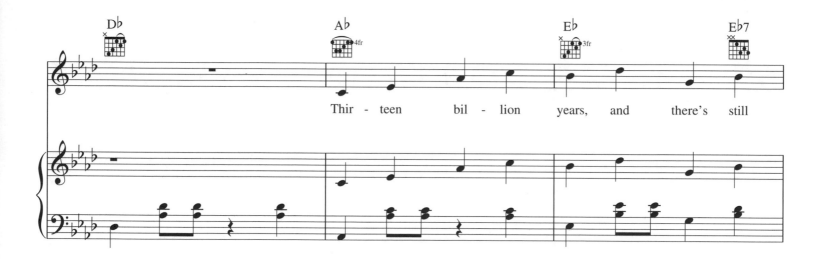

Thir - teen bil - lion years, and there's still

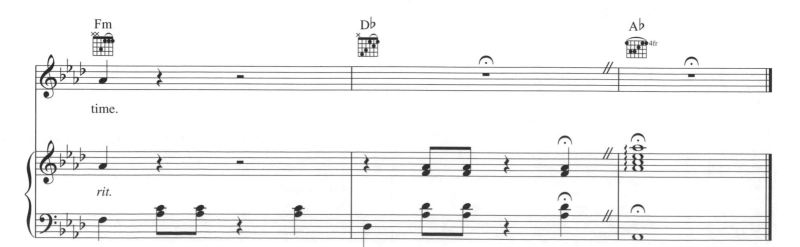

time.

rit.